Berlitz

hide
this
spanish
book101

Berlitz Publishing
New York   Munich   Singapore

Hide This Spanish Book 101

Contacting the Editors
Every effort has been made to provide accurate information in this publication, but changes are inevitable. The publisher cannot be responsible for any resulting loss, inconvenience or injury. We would appreciate it if readers would call our attention to any errors or outdated information by contacting Berlitz Publishing, 193 Morris Avenue, Springfield, NJ 07081, USA. email: comments@berlitzbooks.com

First Printing: Spring 2006
Printed in China

ISBN 981-246-761-0

Writer: Isabel Mendoza
Editorial Director: Sheryl Olinsky Borg
Senior Editor/Project Manager: Lorraine Sova
Assistant Editor: Emily Bernath
Production Manager: Elizabeth Gaynor
Cover and Interior Design: Blair Swick, Wee Design Group
Illustrations: Kyle Webster, Amy Zaleski

101
best Spanish expressions

table of contents

*Hide This Spanish Book **101*** is the ultimate collection of Spanish phrases and expressions. It's a countdown of the coolest language—from what's trendy to what's taboo. In addition to the **101** very best expressions, check out the ^{the}**A**_{-list}, which highlights the lingo you've gotta know. But don't stop there—look for 🌡 and 🌡 , which tip you off to the hottest—that is, most vulgar—language. Add 'em all together and you get a ton of *chevére*, cool, Spanish.

intro

Warning: This language can get you into trouble. If you wanna say it in public, that's up to you. But we're not taking the rap (like responsibility and liability) for any problems you could encounter by using the expressions in *Hide This Spanish Book 101*. These include, but are not limited to, verbal and/or physical abuse, bar brawls, cat fights, arrest…. Use caution when dealing with Spanish that's hot!

intro

the basics

¡Quiay!

keeayee

What's up?

This is the fast way to say "¿Qué hay?"

the basics

¿Cómo andas?
<u>ko</u>mo <u>ahn</u>dahs

How're you doing?

Say it with a fresh, relaxed attitude.

the basics

¿Entonces qué?

ehn<u>ton</u>sehs keh

What's happening?

Use this with good friends only.

the basics

4

¿Qué más de tu vida?

keh mahs deh too <u>bee</u>dah

How's life?

Pretty good, huh?!

the basics

¡Quiubo, huevón!
keewbo wehbon

What's going on, big balls?

It's how Chilean guys say hi.

the basics

6

¿Qué fue, cómo está la verga?

keh fweh <u>ko</u>mo eh<u>stah</u> lah <u>behr</u>gah

How's it hanging?

Said by male friends in Venezuela.

¡Sabelotodo!

sahbehlo<u>to</u>do

Smart ass!

Go ahead—offend someone.

the basics

¡Compadre! ¡Comadre!

kom<u>pah</u>dreh   ko<u>mah</u>dreh

Bro! Sis!

*Make someone feel
like part of the family.*

the basics

¡Oiga, hermano!
oy-gah ehrmahno

Hey, bro!

Another casual way to get someone to notice you.

¡Huevón! / ¡Huevoncito!
wehbon / wehbonseeto

Dick!

Literally: Big balls! / Little big balls!

These are nasty little insults.

the basics

the **A**-list

Chao. cha-oh
Bye.

Me piro. meh peero
I'm outta here.

Hasta luego. ahstah lwehgo
See you later.

Hasta lueguito. ahstah lweh-geeto
See you a little later.

Ahí nos vemos. ahee nos behmos
See you.

Bueno, me piro.

bwenoh meh peero

Well, I'm outta here.

the basics

Ahí nos vemos. ¡Chao!

ah<u>ee</u> nos <u>beh</u>mos cha-oh

See you. Bye!

the basics

the scoop

"Cabrón", a widely-used insult, has a variety of meanings: son of a bitch, bastard, and two-timer, just to name a few. Even though this word is extremely vulgar throughout most of South America, it has a very different meaning in Mexico. Guys often use the term "cabrón" to address their good friends, without any offense at all.

the basics

romance

13

¿Estás solo♂?
ehs<u>tah</u>s <u>so</u>lo

¿Estás so♀la?
ehs<u>tah</u>s <u>so</u>lah

Are you alone?

romance

¿Quieres tomar algo?

keeyeh-rehs tomahr ahlgo

Can I buy you a drink?

If he or she is hot, why not?!

romance

15

¿Por qué tan solito♂?

por keh tahn so<u>lee</u>to

¿Por qué tan solita♀?

por keh tahn so<u>lee</u>tah

Why are you so lonely?

romance

¿Bailamos?
buy<u>lah</u>mos

Wanna dance?

Dancing is a popular pastime—
you're certain to get a yes, "sí"!

romance

17

¡Lárguese!
lahrgehseh

Go away!

Not interested?!

romance

18

¡No moleste!

no mol<u>eh</u>steh

Don't be a pest!

A brutal, no-nonsense way to
refuse a come-on.

romance

¡Déjeme en paz!
dehkhemeh ehn pahs

Leave me alone!

Literally: Leave me in peace!

*Rest assured, that guy or girl won't
bother you again if you use this rejection.*

romance

De ninguna manera, ¿qué le pasa?

deh neen<u>goo</u>nah mah<u>neh</u>rah

keh leh <u>pah</u>sah

No way! What's wrong with you?

You'd rather be by yourself

than with that loser!

romance

21

Bésame.

behsahmeh

Kiss me.

Need some TLC?

romance

22

Dame un beso.
dahmeh oon behso

Give me a kiss.

Get physical.

23

Estoy arrecha, cariño.
ehs<u>toy</u> ah<u>rreh</u>chah kah<u>ree</u>nyo

I'm feeling horny, honey.

Gotta be honest about your feelings, right?!

romance

¿Tienes…?
teeyeh-nehs

condones
kondonehs

forros
forros
Literally: covers

capuchas
kahpoochahs
Literally: hoods

impermeables
eempehrmehah-blehs
Literally: raincoats

Do you have condoms?

24

¿Tomas la píldora?

tomahs lah peeldorah

Are you on the pill?

romance

¡No! Es mejor que te pongas un forro.

no ehs meh<u>khor</u> keh
teh <u>pon</u>gahs oon <u>f</u>orro

No! You'd better use a condom.

romance

27

¿Eres gay?
ehrehs gey

Are you gay?

What a loaded question...

romance

Ella juega a los dos bandos.

ehyah hwehgah ah los dos bahndos

She swings both ways.

Literally: She plays on both teams.

romance

the A-list

the best pet names

cariño kahreenyo
honey

mi vida mee beedah
my life

mi amor mee ahmor
my love

mi cielo mee seeyeh-lo
my sky

mami ♀ / papi ♂ 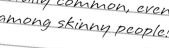 mahmee / pahpee
honey

Literally: mommy / daddy

gordo gordo
fat man

*Totally common, even
among skinny people!*

¡Tremendo bizcocho / bombón!

trehmehndo beeskocho / bombon

Totally cute!

Literally: Tremendous cupcake / bonbon!

The diminutives "bizcochito" and "bomboncito" are also terms of endearment.

romance

¡Es una coqueta!

ehs oonah kokehtah

She's a flirt!

Know anyone like this?

romance

31

Ese tipo es un avión.

ehseh <u>tee</u>poh ehs oon ahvee<u>ohn</u>

That guy is so aggressive.

Literally: That guy's an airplane.

He's only thinking about one thing, huh?!

romance

¿Te mandaron a freir espárragos?

teh mahn-<u>dah</u>ron ah fre<u>heer</u> eh<u>spah</u>rrah-gohs

Were you dumped?

Literally: Were you sent to fry asparagus?

romance

lookin' good

¡Qué buena pinta!

keh <u>bweh</u>nah <u>peen</u>tah

You look great!

Thanks!

lookin' good

Te ves bien con esa pinta.

teh behs beeyehn kon ehsah peentah

That's a good look for you.

You've got style...

lookin' good

¿Le gustaría ir de compras?

leh goostah<u>ree</u>ah eer deh <u>kom</u>prahs

Would you like to go shopping?

Get that cool Latino look.

lookin' good

36

Estos pantalones están "in" / "out".

ehstos pahntahloh-nehs ehstahn in / out

These pants are "in"/ "out".

Make sure your clothes are trendy!

lookin' good

bluyines
blooyeenehs

yins
yeens

pantalones de mezclilla
pahntahloh-nehs deh mehskleeyah
Mexico

vaqueros
bahkehros
Spain

37 jeans

However you call 'em,
jeans are always cool.

38

¡Dios santo, cúbrete!

deeyos <u>sahnto</u> <u>koobrehteh</u>

My God! Cover yourself!

lookin' good

¿Qué haces desnudo?

keh ahsehs dehsnoodo

What are you doing naked?

lookin' good

40

¡Qué tatuaje más chévere!

keh tahtoo<u>ah</u>-kheh mahs <u>cheh</u>behreh

What a cool tattoo!

Oh, really?!

lookin' good

Él tiene un piercing en un pezón.

ehl <u>teeyeh</u>-neh oon <u>peerseeng</u> ehn oon peh<u>son</u>

He has a nipple piercing.

That must've hurt.

lookin' good

Carolina tiene tremendo culo.

kahro<u>lee</u>nah <u>teeyeh</u>-neh treh<u>mehn</u>do <u>koo</u>lo

Carolina has a great butt.

Commenting on someone's "culo" should always be done with discretion.

lookin' good

Andrés tiene un buen bulto.

ahndrehs teeyeh-neh oon bwehn boolto

Andrés has a good package.

How do you know?!

lookin' good

44

Hernán tiene algunos rollitos.

ehr<u>nahn</u> <u>teeyeh</u>-neh ahl<u>goo</u>nos ro<u>yee</u>tos

Hernán has lovehandles.

Poor guy…

lookin' good

Ana nada de espalda y nada de pecho.

ahnah nahdah deh ehspahldah ee nahdah deh pehcho

Ana is flat, back and front.

Literally: Ana swims the backstroke and breaststroke. "Nada" means swim, but it also means nothing... get it?!

lookin' good

46

Voy a hacer pipí / chichí.

boy ah ah<u>sehr</u> pee<u>pee</u> / chee<u>chee</u>

I am going to pee.

Thanks for the announcement.

lookin' good

Voy a hacer del cuerpo.

boy ah ah<u>sehr</u> dehl <u>kwehr</u>po

I'm going to poop.

"Cuerpo" means body... enough said?!

lookin' good

¡Alguien se tiró un pedo!

ahlgeeyehn seh teero oon pehdo

¡Alguien se tiró un gas!

ahlgeeyehn seh teero oon gahs

Someone farted!

Nasty!

lookin' good

Ese tipo tiene aliento de dragón.

ehseh teepo teeyeh-neh ahleeyehn-toh deh drahgon

That guy has dragon breath.

Feel free to substitute "alcantarilla" for "dragón", which means drain breath.

lookin' good

50

¡Estás cadavérico!
ehstahs kahdahveriko

You look like shit!

Literally: You look cadaverous!

lookin' good

havin' fun

the A-list

the best ways to say "fiesta", party

rumba <u>roombah</u>

Colombia

pari pahree

Dominican Republic

heuvadilla <u>wehbahdeeyah</u>

Ecuador

bacanal bahkah<u>nahl</u>

Nicaragua

farra <u>fahrrah</u>

Spain

¡Vamos a parrandear!

<u>bah</u>mos ah pahrrahndeh-<u>ahr</u>

Let's party!

What are you in the mood for?

havin' fun

52

¿Conoces una buena discoteca?

konosehs oonah bwehnah deesko-tehkah

Do you know a good dance club?

He or she is certain to point you in the right direction—maybe even join you!

havin' fun

53

¿Hay un club nocturno en el pueblo?
eye oon kloob nok<u>toor</u>no ehn ehl <u>pweh</u>blo

Is there a nightclub in town?

You're bound to find a good one in just about every Spanish-speaking city!

havin' fun

54

Esta noche quiero beber.

ehstah nocheh keeyeh-ro behbehr

I want to drink tonight.

You've got an exciting evening ahead of you!

havin' fun

Vamos a tomar un trago.

bahmos ah tomahr oon trahgo

Let's have a drink.

Choose from beer, wine, cocktails, shots—Latin American bars and clubs have 'em all!

havin' fun

the A-list

the best ways to say "beer"

una cerveza <u>oo</u>nah sehr<u>beh</u>sah

una chela <u>oo</u>nah <u>cheh</u>lah

Mexico

una birra <u>oo</u>nah <u>beer</u>rah

Bolivia, Chile, Ecuador, Mexico,
Nicaragua, Peru

una fría <u>oo</u>nah <u>free</u>ah

Colombia, Guatemala, Mexico,
Panama, Puerto Rico, Venezuela

una pola _oonah polah_

Colombia

una rubia _oonah roobeeyah_

Costa Rica, Peru

una biela _oonah beeyehlah_

Ecuador

una birria _oonah beerreeyah_

El Salvador

56

¡Salud!
sah<u>lood</u>

Cheers!

Start your night of drinking with a toast

havin' fun

¡Fondo blanco!

fondo blahnko

Bottoms up!

Drink up!

havin' fun

58

José anda empinando el codo.

hoseh ahndah ehmpeenahndo ehl kodo

José is drinking [alcohol].

Literally: José is raising the elbow.

havin' fun

59

María bebe como una esponja.

mah<u>ree</u>ah <u>beh</u>beh <u>ko</u>mo <u>oo</u>nah ehs<u>pon</u>khah

María is a heavy drinker.

Literally: María drinks like a sponge.

havin' fun

Paco ha bebido como bestia.

pa<u>h</u>ko ah beh<u>bee</u>do komo <u>behs</u>teeyah

Paco drinks like a beast.

Someone's gonna have
a monster hangover!

havin' fun

Tengo resaca.

tehngo reh<u>sah</u>kah

I have a hangover.

Sucks to be you!

havin' fun

the scoop

If you're about to go out for a night on the town, but don't want to suffer with a hangover the next day, try this Latino concoction before you start drinking (there's no guarantee this will work for everyone): Swallow two tablespoons of olive oil then two tablespoons of sugar. Follow with a big glass of water. Now you're ready to party!

havin' fun

¿Te molesta si fumo?

teh mol<u>eh</u>stah see <u>foo</u>mo

Do you mind if I smoke?

Puffing up is still a popular pastime for many...

havin' fun

Dora fuma como puta encarcelada. ♀

dorah foomah komo pootah ehnkahrseh-lahdah

Dora is a chain smoker.

Literally: Dora smokes like a whore in jail.
Said in Colombia.

havin' fun

the A-list

the best ways to say "cigarette"

cigarrillo seegahrreeyo

faso fahso
Argentina

pucho poocho
Argentina, Chile, Colombia
Literally: bit

cáncer kahnsehr
Peru   Literally: cancer

pitillo peeteeyo
Spain   Literally: tube

Even though lighting up is still popular throughout Latin America and Europe, some Spanish-speaking countries such as Chile, Honduras, Mexico, Panama, Peru, Spain, and Uruguay have ratified the World Health Organization's Framework Convention on Tobacco Control. That means it's getting harder and harder for cigarette companies to advertise their products; they'll also have to print warning labels on all packaging. And, steps have been taken to protect people from second-hand smoke in indoor workplaces and some indoor public places. You can breathe a little easier now.

¡Juguemos!
hoo<u>geh</u>mos

Let's play!

Get active already!

havin' fun

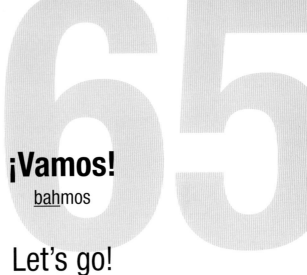

¡Vamos!

<u>bah</u>mos

Let's go!

Scream this during a sporting event.

havin' fun

66

¡Hágale!
<u>ah</u>gahleh

Go!

Push your team to keep goin'!

havin' fun

67

¡A ganar!
ah gahnahr

Go for it!

*Shout this to motivate
your favorite player.*

havin' fun

68

¡Métasela duro!

meh<u>tah</u>sehlah <u>doo</u>ro

Give it to them!

Literally: Stick it hard!

havin' fun

69

¡Duro con ellos!
dooro kon ehyos

Show no mercy!

Literally: Be rude to them!

havin' fun

70

¡Vendido!

behn<u>dee</u>do

You took a bribe!

Literally: Paid for!

havin' fun

¡Sáquelo!

<u>sah</u>kehlo

Kick him out!

Yell this at the referee.

havin' fun

72

¡Pítele!

<u>peet</u>ehleh

Foul!

Literally: Whistle at him!

havin' fun

¡Así no es!
ahs<u>ee</u> no ehs

What the hell is that?!

Did someone just make a bad move?

havin' fun

74

¡Mucha señorita!

moochah sehnyoreetah

You throw like a girl!

Literally: What a Miss!

havin' fun

¡Vaya por la puta bola!

bahyah por lah pootah bolah

Go get the @#&!ing ball!

Sometimes you have to swear.

havin' fun

76

Estoy completamente molido.

ehs<u>toy</u> komplehtah-<u>mehn</u>teh mol<u>ee</u>do

I'm totally worn-out.

Literally: I'm totally ground-up.

havin' fun

¡Estoy sudando a chorros!

ehs<u>toy</u> soo<u>dahn</u>do ah <u>chor</u>ros

The sweat is pouring out of me!

What a workout...

havin' fun

78

¿Hay un casino en el pueblo?

eye oon kah<u>see</u>no ehn ehl <u>pweh</u>blo

Is there a casino in town?

In many Latin American countries, casinos are swanky locales filled with wealthy, well-dressed people.

havin' fun

¿Dónde queda la pista de carreras?

dondeh kehdah lah peestah deh kahrrehrahs

Where's the racetrack?

Got a good tip on a winner?

havin' fun

80

Vamos a jugar a las máquinas tragamonedas.

bahmos ah khoogahr ah lahs mahkeenahs trahgah-monehdahs

Let's play the slot machines.

Are you ready with your bucketful of pesos or euros?

havin' fun

¿Dónde puedo hacer una apuesta?

dondeh pwehdo ahsehr oonah ahpwehstah

Where can I place a bet?

Got money to burn?

havin' fun

82

Le apuesto 200 pesos al 5.
leh ah<u>pwehs</u>to dos-<u>seeyehn</u>tos <u>peh</u>sos ahl <u>seen</u>ko

I'll bet 200 pesos on number 5.

Feeling lucky?

havin' fun

83

¡Gané!
gahneh

I won!

Good for you!

havin' fun

84

¡Me saqué la lotería!

meh sah<u>keh</u> lah lote<u>hree</u>ah

I won the lotto!

What are the chances...

havin' fun

¡Qué partidazo!

keh pahrtee-<u>dah</u>so

What a game!

Had that much fun, huh?!

havin' fun

86

¡Me han estafado!
meh ahn ehstahfahdo

¡Me tumbaron!
meh toombahron

I've been scammed!

You just can't get a break...

havin' fun

Estoy salado.
eh<u>stoy</u> sah<u>lah</u>do

I'm never lucky.

Literally: I'm salted.

havin' fun

¡Malditos!
mahl<u>dee</u>tos

Damn!

Swear only when you need to...

havin' fun

¡Hijueputa!

eekhweh-<u>poo</u>tah

Son of a bitch!

You must be really annoyed
to use this one...

havin' fun

The Scoop

In many Spanish-speaking countries, gambling in casinos, social clubs, racetracks, and stadiums is prohibited for those under 18. However, arcades usually have slot machines, "tragamonedas" or "tragaperras" (Spain), which are often played by teens. People under 18 can also gamble in arcades for minors only. You don't win money, but you do get more tokens to continue playing or tickets that can be exchanged for items such as stuffed toys, posters, stationery, or CDs.

havin' fun

Dame tu e-mail.

<u>dah</u>meh too ee-<u>meyeel</u>

Give me your e-mail.

Hook up with someone new.

tech talk

91

¿Puedo bajar música?
pwehdo bahkhahr mooseekah

Can I download music?

For free?!

tech talk

¿Dónde está el punto de acceso inalámbrico más cercano?

dohndeh ehstah ehl poontoh deh ahksehsoh
eenahlahm-breeko mahs sehrkahno

Where is the closest hotspot?

Meaning Wi-Fi® area...

tech talk

komotás? (¿Cómo estás?)

How RU? (How are you?)

*No need to use opening "¿" and "¡"
in Spanish chat rooms, email messages,
and text messages.*

tech talk

nonetás? (¿Dónde estás?)

Where RU? (Where are you?)

Capitalization is up to you.

tech talk

bss (besos)

xxx (kisses)

How cute!

tech talk

tqm (Te quiero mucho.)

luv u (I love you [very much].)

*Share your feelings in just
a few keystrokes.*

tech talk

97

grax! (¡Gracias!)
TNX (Thanks!)

de nax! (¡De nada!)
UR welcome! (You're welcome!)

Quick ways to be polite...

tech talk

dnd vams? (¿Dónde vamos?)
Where should we go?

disc (discoteca)
dance club

Have fun!

tech talk

the A-list

tech words you've gotta know

conectarse konek-tarseh
to connect

eliminar ehlee-meenahr
to delete

bajar / descargar
bahar / dehs-kahgahr
to download

imprimir eempreemeer
to print